Ta

Bulbs for Spring

Taylor's Pocket Guide to

Bulbs
for Spring

ANN REILLY
Consulting Editor

A Chanticleer Press Edition
Houghton Mifflin Company
Boston

Based on Taylor's Encyclopedia of Gardening, Fourth Edition,
Copyright © 1961 by Norman Taylor,
revised and edited by
Gordon P. DeWolf, Jr.

Prepared and produced by Chanticleer Press, New York
Typeset by Dix Type, Inc., Syracuse, New York
Printed and bound by
Dai Nippon, Tokyo, Japan

Library of Congress Catalog Card Number: 88-46142
ISBN: 0-395-51018-X

00   10   9   8   7   6   5   4   3   2   1

CONTENTS

GARDENING WITH
BULBS FOR SPRING

THE BULBS THAT bloom in spring are among nature's most magical creations—self-contained packages of foliage and flowers that appear, seemingly out of nowhere, to reward you with color year after year. Their beauty in the landscape is dependable and relatively permanent. Planted in the fall, they are triggered into growth the following spring by time or temperature. Spring-blooming bulbs are the most reliable of plants, welcoming the new year of growth often before any other sign of life stirs in the garden.

Bulbs and Bulblike Structures

The plants that we call bulbs have in common the ability to store all of the food they need for growth in a compact package. Although this group of plants actually includes several different types—true bulbs, corms, tubers, tuberous roots, and rhizomes—such plants are usually lumped together as "bulbs" for simplicity's sake. This book includes true bulbs, corms, and tubers, which for all intents and purposes are treated in the same way in the garden. The ability to store food makes these plants well suited to horticulture, for bulbs are durable, easy to handle, and sure to bloom unless they are badly mistreated.

Before setting out to plant your garden, it is wise to learn to distinguish among bulbs and the various bulblike forms.

Doing this will help you plan your garden better and to maintain it well.

A **true bulb** is an enlarged and modified bud. Daffodils, lilies, hyacinths, Glory-of-the-Snow, tulips, and many others are true bulbs. Within the bulb are the future roots, stems, leaves, and flowers, surrounded by fleshy scales that contain all the food necessary for the bulbs to grow. Bulbs are usually covered with a thin, brown, papery covering, like the skin of an onion. After a bulb has bloomed, leaves manufacture the food for the next season and transfer it to the underground portion to start the cycle again.

As bulbs grow, tiny bulblets are formed around their bases. These bulblets can be separated from the main bulb to form new plants. Some bulbs produce small bulbils in the flowers or along their stems that can be used for propagation.

Corms, which include crocus and Dogtooth Violet, are modified solid stems swollen with food storage tissue. At the top is a bud that produces the flowers and leaves, while on the sides are lateral buds that may form small offsets called cormels. A corm is an annual structure: all of its stored food is used to produce flowers and seeds and to begin the growth of new replacement corms that will come to life the following year. Corms are usually short and squat, and covered with a meshlike material.

Tubers, which include Grecian Windflowers, cyclamen, and Winter Aconite, are underground food-storing stems that bear one or more buds on the upper surface. They increase in size every year and may be divided.

Planning the Bulb Landscape

Nothing says "spring" better than a beautiful bulb display. Long before perennials and flowering trees or shrubs have shown a hint of color, spring bulbs such as Winter Aconite, Snowdrops, and early iris appear. Some bloom so early that they turn up amidst the last snows of winter.

Early-blooming spring bulbs such as Siberian Squill, *Puschkinia,* or Glory-of-the-Snow can be planted in the lawn, where they appear before the grass has started to grow. After blooming, they become naturalized. Other bulbs appear with the spring-blooming shrubs and trees, and can be chosen to bloom at the same time for complementary color harmonies. These bulbs include Grape-Hyacinths, hyacinths, and daffodils. Late-blooming alliums add an accent to early perennials and tie the seasons together.

Bulbs can be planted in borders along the path to the front door or the garage. Tiny ones are perfect in rock gardens. Cyclamen and Star-of-Bethlehem do well in woodland gardens, while tulips and hyacinths are effective in mass plantings in formal gardens. You can give your ground covers color and interest in the spring by interplanting them with bulbs. In general, you will want to plant small bulbs near the house, where you can see them better.

Sketch out your garden in advance on paper, indicating the position and color of trees and shrubs. Doing so will allow you to design your garden for maximum succession of bloom and color harmony, and assist you in knowing how many bulbs to buy.

Formal or Informal?

Your taste—as reflected in the style of your home and the rest of your garden—will determine which planting style you will use. Formal gardens are more symmetrical and generally include large blocks of the same color. Bulbs are good plants for formal, geometric patterns. Informal plantings are less planned, and more natural in look, with many different colors of bulbs planted in drifts.

You may want to plant a garden of only one color, a monochromatic garden, and tie it in to the colors of your flowering trees and shrubs. Or you may wish to use complementary colors—for example, planting purple crocus around a pink shrub, or red tulips with blue Grape-Hyacinths.

Choose a variety of bulbs so you will have color in the garden from very early in spring until it is time for summer-blooming perennials and annuals to take over. Annuals can be planted in the empty spaces left by bulbs after they have faded, and they do no harm to the bulbs.

Getting Started

Few gardening experiences match the magic and ease of planting bulbs. Whether you have a large garden or a small one, or even just a sunny windowsill, there are countless bulbs you can grow successfully. Follow a few simple rules, and you can have spectacular color from early spring into summer.

Tender and Hardy Bulbs

All of the structures known collectively as bulbs are either tender or hardy, designations that determine how you treat them in the garden. Tender bulbs cannot withstand freezing temperatures in the ground and must be lifted in fall and stored indoors over winter, except in tropical or subtropical climates. Some tender bulbs are best grown as container plants, especially in the North.

Hardy bulbs are those that withstand cold ground temperatures in winter and actually need the period of cold during their dormancy. In the North, most are grown in the garden like perennials—that is, left in the ground all winter. In climates where winters are warm, hardy bulbs will not grow successfully if left in the ground over winter since temperatures may never drop low enough to induce the dormancy the plant requires. In warm areas, hardy bulbs must be dug in the fall and stored over winter in a refrigerator.

Hardiness Zones

Most of the spring-flowering bulbs discussed in this book are hardy bulbs. The U.S. Department of Agriculture has divided North America into ten climatic zones, based on minimum winter temperatures. Refer to the zone map on pages 106–107 to see which hardiness zone you live in. The zone map should be used as a guideline in handling your bulbs. In each bulb account, a hardiness zone is given, corresponding to the average winter minimum that the bulb will tolerate. It is possible for a bulb to survive and flower at least one hardiness zone colder than indicated if it is planted in a warm, sheltered spot in well-drained soil, and mulched over the winter. If your climate is more than one hardiness zone colder than indicated, or if the conditions are not perfect, you can still grow the bulbs, but it will be necessary to dig them in the fall and store them indoors over the winter.

Choosing a Site

Bulbs need well-drained soil; most prefer full sun. When choosing a planting site, keep in mind temperature variations of different situations. For example, it is colder at the bottom of a hill than it is on a hillside. A depression may not be a good site for bulbs; any that are hardy there will bloom later than bulbs in the rest of the garden. Remember also that many bulbs appear and bloom before the leaves are on the trees; so planting these bulbs under trees may be perfectly acceptable, because they will receive the sunlight they need. You should provide protection from north and west winds.

A Spring Bulb Planting

An ideal location for a bed of most spring bulbs is at the top of a slope, next to a south-facing house foundation. The house protects the plants from north and west winds, the foundation radiates heat and helps the sun to warm the soil, and the slope ensures that cold air will drain away from the area. These optimal conditions will hasten a bulb's growth. You can grow spring-flowering bulbs in perennial flower beds and borders, provided they receive adequate sunlight. If the areas are exposed, bloom time will be later.

Once they are in bloom, spring bulbs are usually not hampered by low air temperatures, although a late snowstorm may damage some flowers or flatten the stems of tall species.

Preparing the Bed

Hardy bulbs are treated like perennials, usually planted in flower beds and borders or shrub borders, where they provide an important part of the total garden picture. Since a perennial bed or border is a major, permanent feature of the garden, it pays to prepare the ground thoroughly in the beginning. The two most important qualities are good drainage and soil that contains an abundance of organic matter, such as compost, well-rotted manure, peat moss, or leaf mold.

Testing the Soil

To test for these qualities, take a handful of moist soil and squeeze it tightly. If water is forced from the soil, it is too wet for plant growth, and you will have to improve the drainage. If the soil retains its shape when you open your hand, it probably contains too high a percentage of clay. If it crumbles, it has too high a proportion of sand. All of these conditions can be corrected by adding organic matter. Draining can be improved with the addition of sharp sand or perlite as well as by adding organic matter. Where severe drainage problems persist, it may be necessary to install drainage tiles underground or to raise the beds.

pH

Most bulbs prefer a soil that is slightly acid to neutral. This is measured by a chemical ratio, called pH, on a scale from 1–14. Neutral soil has a pH of 7; those with a lower pH are acid, and those with a pH over 7 are alkaline. You can ascertain the pH of your soil by having it tested at a soil lab, by the Cooperative Extension Association, or by using a test kit available at garden centers. The pH for most bulbs should be 6.0–7.5; if it needs adjusting, you can raise it with lime or lower it by adding sulfur.

Working the Soil

For bulbs, your soil should be improved to a depth of 12 inches, possibly deeper if you are adding perennials as well. If you are preparing a new area, remove all grass, weeds, roots, and debris from the soil. Cover the area with 3–6 inches of organic matter, adjust the pH if necessary, and add an all-purpose fertilizer according to label directions. Mix the soil and the additional components together with a spade or roto-tiller and rake the surface smooth. Watering with a sprinkler will help to settle the bed. If you are adding bulbs to existing beds, you should improve the soil if this has not been done in a long time.

Buying Bulbs

You can purchase bulbs at your local garden center or from mail-order catalogues. Spring-flowering bulbs are sold in the fall. Be sure bulbs are large, firm, and free of any rot or mold. Be wary of inexpensive bulb collections; small bulbs produce small and often disappointing flowers. It is best to start with large bulbs that will last for many years and produce a more satisfying display.

Planting Bulbs

Most spring-flowering bulbs are planted in the fall. The smaller the bulb and the earlier it flowers in spring, the earlier it should be planted. Plant small bulbs as soon as possible after you purchase them; larger bulbs, such as tulips, hyacinths, and daffodils, can wait until mid-fall or late fall, but must be planted before the ground freezes.

If you cannot plant your bulbs right away, store them in a dark, dry, cool (but not freezing) area, such as the garage or basement. Tubers of Winter Aconite and Grecian Windflower, if they appear to be dried out, should be soaked in water overnight before planting.

If you are planting a large bed, it is easier to dig out the whole bed to the proper depth, put the bulbs in place, and cover them with soil. If you are planting small groups of bulbs, you can dig individual holes with a narrow trowel or a special bulb-planting tool. For good root growth, place bone meal or superphosphate in the bottom of the hole, following label directions. Return the soil to the hole and tamp it down gently.

After planting, water well. One watering should be enough until growth starts in spring. It is wise to mulch new bulb plantings with leaves, straw, salt hay, or evergreen boughs, especially if the bulbs are marginally hardy. In spring, remove the mulch as soon as growth starts. Not removing mulch in time causes foliage to be yellow and may smother the flowers of low-growing varieties.

Planting Depth and Distance

Throughout the bulb descriptions, an approximate planting depth is given; this depth is measured from the bottom of the bulb to the soil line. For all bulbs, a good rule of thumb to find planting depth is to measure the diameter of the bulb, and then multiply this figure by two and one-half or three. The planting distance between bulbs given in the bulb descriptions is measured from center to center.

Placement

Bulbs almost alway look best planted in clusters or groups, not lined up single file across the front of the border. The larger the group or cluster, the better the show. Plant large bulbs in groups of three or more; plant smaller bulbs in groups of a dozen. When they bloom, these clusters usually look best if they are the same color and the same variety.

If you want a naturalistic look, toss the bulbs gently to the ground and plant them where they have fallen, making minor modifications if two fall too closely together. In formal beds, bulbs can be planted in a straight line, but plant them at least three lines deep for the best effect.

Fighting Animal Pests

Chipmunks, rabbits, and other animals find some bulbs an irresistible delicacy during winter. To combat their intrusions, place a layer of fine chicken wire over the planting bed and secure it at the edges, or make a cage out of chicken wire, place the bulbs in the cage, and plant the whole thing. Dusting bulbs with the fungicide Thiram leaves an odor that rodents do not like. Most animals will not bother *Narcissus* bulbs. Some animals, particularly squirrels, chew off tulip flowers when they bloom; there is little you can do to dissuade them, except to plant a different type of bulb. Some gardeners recommend using blood meal or moth balls as a deterrent, but these have limited value, and their effectiveness is reduced after watering or rain.

Caring for Spring Bulbs

On the whole, bulbs require comparatively little attention from the gardener. But no plants do well if they are neglected. For best results with your spring-blooming bulbs, there are a few simple guidelines you should follow.

Fertilizer and Water

Bulbs like moderately fertile soil. To keep them growing and flowering well, fertilize them lightly every year when growth starts or when the flowers start to fade. Spread the fertilizer evenly over the soil, scratch it in lightly, and water. For advice on what kind of fertilizer to use, consult with your local garden specialist or nurseryman.

When they are in growth, bulbs need an evenly moist soil. Water deeply if there are no spring rains.

Foliage and Flowers

After a bulb's flowers fade, the foliage will start to ripen— that is, to manufacture and store food for the following year. In this process, the leaves sometimes show increased growth. In all bulbs, the foliage will turn yellow, then brown, and finally die. It is very important not to remove any foliage until after it has fully ripened. If the foliage is unattractive, you may want to curl it up, braid it, or hide it under a nearby plant. If bulbs are growing in the lawn, do not mow the grass until the foliage has ripened.

Remove flowers as soon as they have faded so the energy of the bulb is not used up in producing seeds, unless you want your bulbs to set seed and self-sow. Tulips, hyacinths, and daffodils generally do not self-sow satisfactorily, so it is best to remove their flowers as soon as they have faded.

Problems with Growth and Blooming

If bulbs fail to come up the first year, they may not be hardy in your region. They may have rotted if the soil was too wet, or they may have been eaten by rodents. Try them again, planting them deeper and providing protection from animals.

If bulbs grow but do not bloom, you may have removed the foliage too early the previous year, making them weak; or you may have started with bulbs that are too small. It is possible with some bulbs to revive them over a year or two by fertilizing and allowing the foliage to ripen completely. In most cases, you'll have more satisfaction if you start over.

Some bulbs that had been productive in the past but are now not blooming to their peak probably are too crowded and need to be divided. Dig them after the flowers fade, divide them, and replant, being careful not to remove the foliage unless it has fully ripened. Bulbs may also be dug and divided immediately after the foliage completely fades or in the fall, but it is often then difficult to find them, and you can damage the bulbs by digging if you don't know exactly where they are.

Tulips and hyacinths naturally become smaller and weaker over time. There is little you can do to reverse this process. When they become ineffective, plant new bulbs.

Mulching

Spring-flowering bulbs do not usually need to be mulched during their growing season. Mulch applied in early spring will actually retard the warming of the soil and will delay growth and flowering. Bulbs planted in perennial beds and borders can be mulched after the flowering is completed; the soil will benefit from being kept cool, weed-free, and moist. Organic mulches will also enrich the soil.

Bulbs will benefit from a winter mulch that keeps the soil temperature constant and prevents heaving of the bulbs from the soil by alternate freezing and thawing. Good organic mulching materials include leaves (especially oak leaves), straw, salt hay, and evergreen boughs.

Storing Bulbs in Winter

Most spring-flowering bulbs can be left in the ground for years. Some, however, are not winter hardy. Others cannot tolerate wet soil or the alternate freezing and thawing of the ground in winter, and a few must have completely dry soil in summer. In warm areas, bulbs must be dug and given a cold treatment over winter to induce dormancy before replanting the following spring. In such cases, the bulbs must be dug and stored until they are replanted; see the individual plant descriptions for details.

It is best to dig the bulbs right after the foliage has ripened, when they are easier to find. They can, however, be dug in fall before frost if you can find them without damaging them.

Dig the bulbs carefully, wash off all soil, allow them to dry, and store them indoors in a box or plastic bag containing dry peat moss. Keep them in a cool, dry, dark area. Check them from time to time. If condensation forms, open the container to allow them to dry out. If the bulbs start to grow, they need a place that is cooler or darker.

If you live in a warm area and your bulbs need to be chilled, store them first in a cool area as you would other bulbs, and then refrigerate them for 12–14 weeks immediately before replanting. Some bulbs that are marginally winter hardy may be dug in the fall and overwintered in containers outdoors in a cold frame. (A cold frame is a bottomless box with a removable, transparent top that traps the heat of the sun's rays while keeping out cold wind.)

Dividing Bulbs

Most bulbs produce small offsets, bulblets, or cormels, which lie crowded around the original bulb. In time, these offsets will compete so much for nutrients and water that blooming will decrease. When this occurs, dig the bulbs carefully after the foliage has faded. Remove the small offsets and replant them. They may not flower the first year after division, but should reach blooming size by the second year, and using offsets is an excellent way to increase your bulb plantings. When digging corms, discard the original, which will die anyway, and replant the cormels.

Tubers can be divided by cutting them with a sharp knife. Be sure there is at least one bud on each division.

Reseeding

It is possible to collect bulb seeds for propagation, but blooming will in most cases have to wait for several years. It is generally easier to start with bulbs or divisions. Some of the tiny bulbs, however, such as squills, Glory-of-the-Snow, and *Puschkinia,* reseed easily, quickly forming large, natural-looking colonies. You need do nothing to help nature along, but remember not to remove flowers until they have completely faded.

Growing Bulbs in Containers

Spring-flowering bulbs that are not hardy are often grown in containers, where they do not have to be dug and replanted every year. You can use containers made of almost any material, provided they are light enough to move indoors and out. Containers must have drainage holes; if you wish to use a decorative pot, plant the bulbs in a pot with drainage holes, and place this pot inside of the other one.

Use a soilless potting medium of peat moss and perlite or vermiculite. Water the potting medium after potting up the bulbs, but do not water again until growth starts. Once that occurs, water regularly so the soil is always moist but not soggy. Fertilize with half-strength houseplant fertilizer every two weeks. After flowering, as the foliage starts to ripen, decrease watering. When the foliage has completely browned, store the bulb in its container in a cool, dry, dark place. Late the following winter, return the container to a warm room, place it in sunlight, and water it to start the cycle again.

Forcing Bulbs Indoors

Many bulbs—especially tulips, hyacinths, crocus, and daffo-dils—can be forced indoors for early bloom. Paper-white nar-cissus, which are very fragrant, are a favorite for forcing.

Plant bulbs singly or in a group in containers. Select a pot twice as deep as the bulbs. Fill it three-quarters full with a soilless potting mix and place the bulbs half an inch apart on top of the medium. Press them into the medium so the tips are even with the top of the pot. Add more medium, until it reaches one-quarter of an inch from the top of the pot. Water it so that the medium is evenly moist.

Place the container in the refrigerator, a cold frame, or out-doors in a trench under a covering of mulch for 12–14 weeks. Bring the pots indoors and place them in indirect sunlight for ten days. Then move them into the sun, avoiding heat and drafts. To provide adequate humidity, set the pots on pebble trays filled with water. Flowers should appear in three to four weeks. Prolong blooming by keeping the plants cool.

After flowers fade, allow foliage to ripen naturally. Paper-white narcissus bulbs should be discarded because they will not satisfactorily bloom again. If you save the bulbs of the other kinds, you can plant them in the garden, where they will bloom the following year; forcing them a second time does not work.

A Note on Plant Names

The common, or English, names of plants are often colorful and evocative, but they vary widely from region to region.

Sometimes two different plants have the same or similar common name; some plants have no English name at all. Fortunately, every plant is assigned a scientific (or Latin) name that is distinct and unique to that plant. Scientific names are not necessarily "better," but they are standard around the world and governed by an international set of rules. Therefore, even though scientific names may at first seem difficult or intimidating, they are in the long run a simple and sure way of getting a handle on the plant you want.

What's In a Name?

A scientific name has two parts. The first is called the generic name: it tells us to which genus (plural, genera) a plant belongs. Sometimes the generic name is the same in Latin and English: *Narcissus*. The second part of the name tells us the species. (A species is a kind of plant or animal that is capable of reproducing with members of its kind, but genetically isolated from others. *Homo sapiens* is a species.) Most genera have many members: *Allium*, for example, has about 400. *Allium caeruleum* is one of the several *Allium* species included in this book. Scientific names are always italicized or underlined; the generic name is always capitalized, and the species name, as a rule, is not (there are exceptions).

The names of naturally occurring varieties are also in italics; they form a third part of the scientific name. The names of cultivars (cultivated varieties, developed by plant breeders) are usually in roman type, enclosed by single quotation marks. They may follow a one- or two-part scientific name, as in *Crocus chrysanthus* 'Blue Pearl' and *Narcissus* 'Lemon Tarts'. Although cultivars and varieties are technically different, they may be treated by the gardener in the same way.

A hybrid is a plant that is the result of a cross between two genera, two species, or two varieties or cultivars. Sometimes hybrids are given a new scientific name, but they are usually indicated by an × within the scientific name. There are many hybrid groups, or classes, featured in this book, in the narcissus and tulips.

Organization of the Plant Accounts

The plant accounts in this book are arranged alphabetically by scientific name. If you know only the common name of a flower, look the plant up in the index under its common name and refer to the page listed.

Some accounts in the book deal with a garden plant at the level of genus, because the genus includes many similar species that are treated in more or less the same way in the garden. In these accounts, only the genus name is given at the top of the page; the name of the species, cultivar, or hybrid pictured is noted within the text.

Ready, Set, Grow!

These are the basic facts you will need to know to bring the magic of spring-blooming bulbs into your landscape. With a little attention, these flowers will bring you delightful color year after year, as dependably as the spring brings new life.

Bulbs for Spring

Blue Allium *(Allium caeruleum)*

Blue Allium is one of the few members of its genus with blue flowers. The round flower clusters are 2–5 inches wide and appear in very late spring on stems 1–2 feet tall. The small bulbils that appear inside of the flower clusters can be used for propagation.

GROWING TIPS

Plant *Allium caeruleum* in full sun i soil that is rich and well drained The soil should be kept moist dur ing the growing season. Plant bulb in mid-spring, 4–6 inches deep an 8 inches apart. Divide in early sum mer only when the clumps becom crowded. The flowers can be drie and are very attractive used in drie arrangements.

This late-spring-blooming bulb is listed in some books and catalogues as *A. albopilosum*. The large, round clusters of flowers are lilac-colored and have a metallic sheen; they grow 8–12 inches across. The flower stalks are 1½–2½ feet tall. The leaves are flat, white, and hairy on the undersides, and 18 inches in length.

GROWING TIPS

Plant Star of Persia in full sun in soil that is rich and well drained. The soil should be kept moist during the growing season. Plant bulbs in mid-spring, 6 inches deep and 8–10 inches apart. Divide in early summer only when the clumps become crowded. The flowering heads dry easily and work very well in dried arrangements.

Giant Garlic *(Allium giganteum)*

This is not the largest-flowered allium, but it is one of the tallest, with flowering stems reaching 3–5 feet tall. Round flower heads are pinkish purple and 4–6 inches across. The leaves are blue-gray, strap-shaped, 2 inches wide and 18 inches long. The foliage often turns brown by the late-spring blooming time, so plant this bulb behind other plants that will hide its base.

Growing Tips

Plant *Allium giganteum* in full sun c partial shade in soil that is rich an well drained. The soil should b kept moist during the growing sea son. Plant bulbs in mid-spring, inches deep and 10–12 inches apart Divide in early summer only whe the clumps become crowded.

Known as Turkestan Allium for the place of its origin, this allium is low-growing and compact. The leaves, which are blue-green, 5 inches wide, and 10 inches long, curve under. The round flower heads are 3–4 inches across; the flowers are silvery pink or white, veined with purple, and appearing lavender from a distance. Flower stems are 6–10 inches tall and appear in late spring as tulips fade.

GROWING TIPS

Plant *Allium karataviense* in full sun in soil that is rich and well drained. The soil should be kept moist during the growing season. Plant bulbs in mid-spring, 4 inches deep and 4–6 inches apart. Divide in early summer only when the clumps become crowded. Like many other alliums, this species has flowers that are attractive in dried arrangements.

Lily Leek *(Allium Moly)*

This decorative species works very well in the rock garden or borders. It grows 12–14 inches tall and has loose clusters of bright yellow, star-shaped flowers. Blooms are 3 inches across and appear in mid- to late May. The flat leaves are 2 inches wide and resemble those of iris. The common name, Lily Leek, reflects this species' relationship to edible garden leeks.

GROWING TIPS

Plant Lily Leek in full sun in so that is rich and well drained. Th soil should be kept moist during th growing season. Plant bulbs in mid spring, 4 inches deep and 4– inches apart. Divide in early sum mer only when the clumps becom crowded.

Daffodil Garlic (*Allium neapolitanum*)

The Daffodil Garlic is one of the first alliums to bloom, appearing in mid-spring. It bears decorative clusters of star-shaped, white, fragrant flowers on 12- to 18-inch stems. Leaves are flat and 1 inch wide, a little shorter than the flower stem. In areas where the plant is not hardy, it may be grown in pots and overwintered in a cold frame.

GROWING TIPS

Plant Daffodil Garlic in full sun in soil that is rich and well drained. The soil should be kept moist during the growing season. Plant bulbs in mid-spring, 4 inches deep and 4–6 inches apart. Divide in early summer only when the clumps become crowded. The flowers can be dried and are very attractive in dried arrangements.

Allium *(Allium Rosenbachianum)*

This is a showy allium, with a flower stalk that grows 2–4 feet tall. The 2 or 3 leaves are much shorter than the stalk, ½–2 inches wide, and smooth. The pinkish-purple flowers bloom in round clusters in late spring. The individual flowers often have a darker stripe in the center of each petal. This species is sometimes known as the Rosenbach Onion.

GROWING TIPS

Plant *Allium Rosenbachianum* in fu sun in soil that is rich and we drained. The soil should be ke moist during the growing seaso Plant bulbs in mid-spring, 6 inch deep and 6–8 inches apart. Divi in early summer only when t clumps become crowded.

Grecian Windflower (*Anemone blanda*)

These low-growing plants are covered in mid-spring with masses of daisylike flowers of blue, pink, or white, with bright yellow centers. The flowers almost hide the starburst-shaped foliage that hugs the ground. Each bloom on this 6-inch plant is 1–2 inches across. Grecian Windflower is best planted in informal gardens, under trees, or in the rock garden. It can also be potted in the fall and forced indoors for late-winter bloom.

GROWING TIPS

Grecian Windflower prefers partial shade but will grow in full sun. Average garden soil, as long as it is fast draining, is sufficient to make a colorful display. The tubers have no top or bottom and should be planted in early fall, 2 inches deep and 4–6 inches apart. If they appear shriveled, soak them in water overnight before planting. These plants rarely if ever need dividing. Foliage disappears quickly after the flowers fade, allowing flowering annuals to be planted easily where the Grecian Windflowers bloomed.

Spanish Hyacinth *(Brimeura amethystina)* Zone

This bulb is still listed in some books by its former name, *Hyacinthus amethystinus*. Named for a 16th-century French gardener, Marie de Brimeur, the species bears individual flowers that look like those of the hyacinth, but appear in loose clusters. The nodding, fragrant flowers are light blue or white and bloom on 4- to 10-inch stems. The narrow, grassy leaves grow to 8 inches high. Blooming in early spring, it is particularly well suited to the rock garden.

GROWING TIPS

Plant Spanish Hyacinth in full su in deep, rich, fertile soil. Plant i early fall to mid-fall, 6 inches dee and 6 inches apart. Apply a protec tive winter mulch of leaves or eve green boughs as soon as the groun has frozen in the fall.

White Globe Lily *(Calochortus albus)*

This plant belongs to a subgroup of the genus *Calochortus* known globe tulips or fairy lanterns. The flowers are white, 1½ inches long, and globe-shaped, like small pearls nodding from slender 2-foot stems. This early spring bloomer is related to the Mariposa Lily, but its flowers are quite different in appearance.

GROWING TIPS

Plant White Globe Lilies in full sun to light shade in poor, light, well-drained soil. Set the corms 2 inches deep and 6 inches apart in early fall to mid-fall. Soil should be kept moist while the corms are growing and dry for the rest of the year. These plants are fairly winter hardy, but do not like alternate freezing and thawing. Therefore, you should apply a deep mulch in late fall as soon as the ground has frozen; do not remove it until growth has started in spring.

Mariposa Lily *(Calochortus)*

Several species within this genus are called Mariposa Lily or Butterfly Tulip. The flowers resemble tulips and bloom in late spring on slender stems surrounded by grassy leaves. Seen here is *C. Gunnisonii*, or Sego Lily, which has white, purple-streaked flowers 1¾ inches long that bloom on 18-inch stems. *C. luteus* has yellow or orange flowers that have brown spots at the base of the petals and brown stripes. Flower stems are 1–2½ feet high.

GROWING TIPS

Plant mariposa lilies in full sun partial shade in poor, sandy, we drained soil. The soil should moist during the growing seas but dry during the summer. If t cannot be achieved, dig the bul after the foliage has browned spring, store them over the summ in a dry place, and replant them fall. In zones 5–7, mulch heavily fall after the ground has started freeze, or dig the bulbs in fall, pla them in pots in a cold frame ov winter, and replant in spring.

Camassias are among the last of the spring bulbs to flower. All ve narrow, grasslike leaves growg from the base of the plant. Erect ikes bear showy blue or white wers with prominent stamens. ctured here is *C. Cusickii,* which s 3½-foot slender spikes of pale ue flowers; *C. Leichtlinii* has 4-foot ikes of blue or white flowers. It orks well in open borders. Camas, Bear Grass *(C. Quamash)* has blue white flowers; Wild Hyacinth *(C. lloides)* has pale blue to white wers.

GROWING TIPS

Camassia grows in full sun or light shade and prefers heavy soil that is moist but well drained. Be sure the plants do not dry out during the growing season. Plant the bulbs 4 inches deep and 4–6 inches apart in fall. They can be left undisturbed for many years and do not need dividing. Foliage disappears quickly after the bulbs bloom.

Glory-of-the-Snow (*Chionodoxa Luciliae*)

These plants received their name because they bloom in late winter, often when there is still snow on the ground. The 1-inch, white-centered, star-shaped flowers have 6 petals and bloom in clusters. Most varieties are blue, although there are also pink forms. Flower stalks grow 3 inches high over grassy foliage. Glory-of-the-Snow is used in rock gardens, under trees and shrubs, and can be planted in the lawn. It combines well with *Puschkinia* and Siberian Squill for an early, all-blue color display. The similar *C. sardensis* has somewhat smaller blue flowers that lack the white eye.

Growing Tips

Plant Glory-of-the-Snow in the fall in full sun or partial shade. Set bulbs 4 inches deep and 3 inches apart, in average to dry soil. The plants never need dividing. Leave faded flowers to reseed and form dense colonies within a few years. Foliage disappears quickly after the flowers fade.

Scotch Crocus *(Crocus biflorus)*

These bulbs are characterized by a stripe on the outside of the petals. The blooms, which are 4 inches high, are white, lilac, or purplish blue and have a yellow throat; the foliage reaches 6 inches in height. Useful for the rock garden, these bloom in early spring. A violet variety, *Adamii,* is one of several named forms. The flowers open in the morning sun and close up in the afternoon.

GROWING TIPS

Crocus like to be grown in full sun or light shade; they do well near deciduous trees, because the leaves have not yet appeared when these flowers bloom. Plant corms in early fall, 3 inches deep and 3–4 inches apart. Soil should be rich, sandy, and well drained. Clumps may become crowded; every 3–5 years, lift and divide them after the foliage has turned brown in spring.

Crocus *(Crocus chrysanthus)*

The flowers of this crocus are sweetly fragrant and pale yellow to orange-yellow. Very narrow leaves grow to 12 inches high, with most of the growth made after the flowers have faded. Bloom time is in early spring. There are many good horticultural forms that resemble Dutch Crocus but have smaller flowers. 'Snow Bunting' is white with a yellow throat; 'Blue Pearl', seen here, is lavender outside and white inside, with a yellow throat; 'E. P. Bowles' is yellow.

GROWING TIPS

Plant corms in early fall, 3 inches deep and 3–4 inches apart. Soil should be rich, sandy, and well drained. Crocus do very well along path edges, as well as at the bases of trees and shrubs. When clumps become crowded, every 3–5 years, lift and divide them after the foliage has turned brown in spring.

rocus *(Crocus Tomasinianus)*

This crocus is among the earliest to bloom in spring. Blooms are ar-shaped, and lilac to purple with yellow to white throat. Unlike any crocuses, this species produces liage at the same time as the flowers. Plants grow to 6 inches.

GROWING TIPS

Plant corms in early fall, 3 inches deep and 3–4 inches apart, in a sunny spot with warm, rich, sandy, well-drained soil. They naturalize well in lawns, but the grass cannot be mowed until the foliage dies down. Crocus do not need to be dug every year, but if clumps become crowded, lift and divide them after the foliage has browns in spring.

Common Crocus (*Crocus vernus*)

Hybrids of the Common Crocus make up the category of the large-flowered Dutch Crocus. The species have white, yellow, or purple flowers that are usually striped on the outside. The Dutch Crocus are available in a variety of solid colors and stripes and are among the last crocus to bloom in early spring. Foliage appears with the flowers but continues to grow after the flowers have faded.

GROWING TIPS

Grow Common Crocus in full s or light shade; they do well lawns, or near deciduous trees, sin leaves do not appear until after the flowers bloom. Plant corms in ea fall, 3 inches deep and 3–4 inch apart. Soil should be rich, sand and well drained. Crocus naturali well in lawns, but the grass cann be mowed until the foliage di down. Every 3–5 years, whe clumps become crowded, lift an divide them after the foliage h turned brown in spring.

Cyclamen (*Cyclamen*)

There are several species of cyclamen that grow well in the rock garden and resemble the cyclamen sold by florists as a houseplant. The leaves are round to kidney-shaped and form at the base of the plant. Seen here is *C. coum*, which grows 3–6 inches high and has flowers of white to carmine with a purple blotch. The leaves are solid green or mottled above and reddish purple on the undersides. The similar *C. repandum* has larger leaves and flowers. Both bloom in early spring to mid-spring.

GROWING TIPS

Plant cyclamen in partial shade in rich, moist, well-drained soil. Plant them during the summer, 2 inches deep and 6–8 inches apart. They require heavy protection during the winter in the northern limits of their hardiness. Where they are not hardy, they may be lifted from the soil in the fall and overwintered in pots in a cold frame. Replant them in spring.

Blue Dicks *(Dichelostemma pulchellum)*

This plant is sometimes called Wild Hyacinth, and is listed in some books as *Brodiaea capitata* or *B. pulchella*. The globe-shaped blooms are made up of violet to white flowers surrounded by colorful, metallic-purple bracts. Flowers bloom on 2-foot stems in early spring. The leaves are nearly round and 16 inches long.

GROWING TIPS

Grow Blue Dicks in full sun in sandy, well-drained soil. Plant them in early fall, 2–3 inches deep and (inches apart. Soil should be mois during the growing season but mus be dry during the summer. Apply heavy protection in winter to avoid alternate freezing and thawing o the soil. Where this method wil not work, lift plants from the ground after the foliage has browned in late spring and store them in a dry place over the summer; in fall place them in pots and overwinter in a cold frame. Replant in spring.

Winter Aconite *(Eranthis hyemalis)*

This early-blooming plant appears in late winter, often showing its waxy, yellow flowers on top of the snow. The flowers bloom on 3-inch stalks above shiny, thick, dark green foliage that forms a star-shaped base for the blossoms. Each 6-petalled, sweet-scented flower is 2 inches across and looks like a large buttercup.

GROWING TIPS

Winter Aconite must be planted as early in the fall as possible. The tuber must never be allowed to dry out and should be set into the ground 2 inches deep; space plants 3–4 inches apart. If the tubers have started to shrivel, soak them overnight in water before planting. Plant in full sun or partial shade under trees or shrubs. The soil must be rich, moist, and well drained, especially in the summer when new roots are forming. Leave undisturbed, and in a few years a well-established colony will develop.

Dogtooth Violet (*Erythronium*)

These flowers are not violets at all, but members of the lily family. The common name comes from the resemblance of the white corm to a dog's tooth; the flowers are also called trout lilies, for their mottled leaves look like a trout's markings. Suitable for the wild-flower garden, dogtooth violets grow 12 inches high and have basal foliage that surrounds the flower stem. *E. americanum,* also called Yellow Adder's Tongue, has yellow flowers with recurved petals. Seen here is *E. Dens-canis*, which has nod-ding, purplish-pink flowers. Bo
bloom in early spring.

GROWING TIPS

Plant dogtooth violets in light t
partial shade in rich, moist soil tha
is neutral to slightly acid. Plar
corms in early fall, 3 inches dee
and 4 inches apart. They can be le
undisturbed for many years. Mulc
with an organic mixture of shredde
leaves or similar material to keep th
soil cool, moist, and rich.

Popular and easy to grow, Crown Imperial bears a tuft of yellow, red, or orange 2-inch flowers under a crown of foliage, all atop a thick, 30- to 48-inch stem. These same lance-shaped leaves clothe the stem about two-thirds of the way up to the flower. The fragrance can be very heavy and sometimes unpleasant. Crown Imperial is a formal plant and combines well with tulips, which bloom at the same time in mid-spring to late spring. Use it as an accent plant rather than in a massed planting.

GROWING TIPS

Crown Imperial likes full sun or light shade and a rich, well-drained soil that is kept moist during spring and summer. Plant 5 inches deep and 12–15 inches apart in early fall. The plants should be dug in spring after the foliage fades or in fall; divide and replant every 4–5 years.

Checker Lily *(Fritillaria lanceolata)*

Also called Mission Bells, this species bears drooping flowers that look like upside-down tulips. The flowers are purple, mottled with greenish; they bloom in early spring on 2-foot stems. The leaves are oval or lance shaped.

GROWING TIPS

Plant Checker Lily in full sun light shade in rich, well-drain soil. Keep the soil moist during t summer but ensure that it is dry a very well drained in winter to pr vent rot. Plant bulbs as early in f as possible, 4 inches deep and inches apart. Lift and divide every or 4 years. Checker Lily is found the wild in the Pacific Northwe and grows best in that region.

uinea-Hen Flower *(Fritillaria Meleagris)*

Closely related to the Checker Lily, this species also has 2-ch, nodding flowers that look like lampshade or an upside-down tip. Guinea-Hen Flower blooms mid-spring. Although there are hite- and yellow-flowered forms, ost are checkered in purple and hite. The blooms appear on 6- to 2-inch wiry stems above rather in, grasslike foliage. Guinea-Hen ower works nicely when it can be en at close range in rock gardens foundation plantings; it is less ef-ctive in mass plantings.

GROWING TIPS

Plant Guinea-Hen Flower in full sun to partial shade. Set the bulbs 4 inches deep and 5 inches apart in rich, well-drained garden soil; keep the soil moist during the summer so the bulbs do not dry out. Plant the bulbs as early in the fall as possible. Every 3–4 years, the bulbs may be lifted, divided, and replanted.

Snowdrops *(Galanthus)*

Snowdrops often bloom when winter's snow is still upon the ground—hence their common name. They have white flowers on a narrow stalk that grows from the center of 2 or 3 basal, grasslike leaves. Two species, *G. byzantinus* and *G. Elwesii,* are quite similar in appearance; the latter, seen here, is known as Giant Snowdrop for its larger flowers, to 1½ inches long, and its longer flowering stalks, which can reach a foot in height. *G. byzantinus* grows 3–9 inches high.

GROWING TIPS

Snowdrops should be planted large groups in light, rich so Since they bloom before the tr leaf out, they can be planted eith under deciduous trees or in mc open areas. They do well in woo land gardens and appreciate a wint mulch of leaves. Plant bulbs inches deep and 2 inches apart early fall. They increase freely a may be left in place for many yea without being divided.

Desert Lily *(Hesperocallis undulata)*

The funnel-shaped, fragrant flowers of Desert Lily are 2½ inches long, and appear in mid-spring in spiked clusters of 10–12 blooms. There is a green stripe on the outside of the petals. The flower stalk, which is leafless, grows to 2½ feet tall; the basal leaves are 18 inches long and ½ inch wide, with crispy white margins.

GROWING TIPS

Desert Lily, as the name implies, needs desert conditions of hot, dry summers and cool, moist winters and springs. Plant bulbs 6 inches deep and 8 inches apart in sandy, well-drained soil. When the plant is not grown in the desert, make sure the soil is moist during the growing period and dry in summer. If these conditions do not exist naturally, you can still grow Desert Lily in containers.

Spanish Bluebells *(Hyacinthoides hispanicus)*   Zone

You may see this plant listed in catalogs as *Scilla campanulata, Scilla hispanica,* or Wood Hyacinth. The flowers, which may be white, blue, or pink, are a cross between the squill and the hyacinth. Nodding blooms appear on 18- to 20-inch spikes and resemble a very loose hyacinth. The flowers appear in late spring and make a pretty complement to late tulips.

GROWING TIPS

Plant Spanish Bluebells in moist rich soil in open borders or unde light, deciduous shade. Set th bulbs in fall, 2 inches deep and 3– inches apart. They can be left i place for many years without bein divided. They may self-sow, an they make abundant offsets, quickl forming attractive colonies. Foliag disappears quickly after the plan blooms in spring.

Common Hyacinth *(Hyacinthus orientalis)* Zone 5

No spring garden is complete without one or more of the many cultivars of the Hyacinth. The dense, thick, stiff flower clusters made up of star-shaped flowers may be white, pink, blue, yellow, purple, or red. All are extremely fragrant. The flowers appear in mid-spring from the center of basal leaves. Hyacinths can be used in either formal or informal gardens and are best planted in groups.

GROWING TIPS

Hyacinths like full sun and deep, rich, fertile soil. Plant them in mid-fall, 6 inches deep and 6 inches apart. Mulch in late fall to protect new growth as it pushes through the soil; growth can be premature during warm spells in winter. After several years, hyacinth flowers will become small and will lose most of their compactness, and should be replaced. Hyacinths may also be forced indoors over the winter in potting medium or in water.

Spring Starflower *(Ipheion uniflorum)*

This plant is often confused with *Brodiaea* and *Triteleia*. It is related to both, and often looks similar, but it blooms in early spring, while the others bloom in summer. The star-shaped flowers are white tinged with blue, and 1½ inches across. They appear on 6- to 8-inch stems that grow from the center of a clump of grass-shaped leaves. If you brush against the leaves, they give off a strong odor of onions.

GROWING TIPS

Plant Spring Starflower in early fall 3 inches deep and 4–6 inches apart. The bulbs need full sun in sandy or gravelly, well-drained soil that is not overly moist. They produce offsets rapidly and form a large colony quickly. Divide whenever they become crowded. Foliage appears in autumn and lasts all winter; protect it with evergreen boughs or leaves. It may turn brown but can be trimmed with scissors.

GROWING TIPS

This is the earliest of the irises to bloom in the spring. It is very small, growing only 4 inches high, so should be located where it can be seen and enjoyed at close range. The bright golden-yellow flowers, 2–3 inches long, appear before the foliage. The grassy leaves start to grow as the flowers fade and can reach a height of 8 inches.

Plant Danford Iris in full sun in rich, moist, well-drained soil. Plant bulbs as early as possible in the fall, 4 inches deep and 3–4 inches apart. They may not be long-lived, as the bulbs often break up into a number of nonflowering bulblets; if you start to notice foliage but no flowers, dig up the bulbs and replace them. Apply a protective mulch of leaves or evergreen boughs over the winter. Danford Iris may also be grown in pots.

Harput Iris (*Iris histrioides*)

Growing just 4–9 inches tall, this tiny bulbous iris is perfect for the small garden or mixed with dwarf conifers for an early spring bloom. The blue flowers are 3 inches across, wider than those of other early-blooming irises. They appear long before the grassy leaves, which can grow to 12 inches long after the flowers fade. 'Major', the cultivar seen here, has bright blue flowers.

GROWING TIPS

Harput Iris should be grown in full sun in sandy, moist, well-drained soil. Plant bulbs in early fall, inches deep and 3–4 inches apart. They benefit from winter protection of leaves or evergreen boughs.

These dainty irises grow best in the rock garden or in clumps near the front door, where their early spring bloom can be enjoyed. The attractive, fragrant flowers, 2–4 inches long, may be blue, violet, or purple, sometimes flecked with yellow on the outer petals. The grasslike foliage, which appears after the flowers have bloomed, grows to a height of 8 inches. 'Harmony', seen here, and 'Violet Beauty' are well-known varieties.

GROWING TIPS

Plant Netted Iris in full sun in rich, moist, well-drained soil. The bulbs, which have a characteristic netting on the outside, should be planted in early fall, 4 inches deep and 3–4 inches apart. They are not long-lived and may need replanting every 3 to 4 years. Mulch with leaves or evergreen boughs over the winter. This species can also be grown in pots.

Spanish Iris *(Iris Xiphium)*

The hybrid descendants of the Spanish Iris, known as Dutch Iris, are more widely grown today than the wild form seen here. These hybrids have large, orchidlike flowers of white, yellow, purple, or blue that bloom in late spring. The flowering stems are 18–24 inches tall and grow in the middle of long, lance-shaped leaves. The hybrid forms are used by florists and are very long-lasting as a cut flower from the garden.

GROWING TIPS

Plant Spanish Iris or Dutch Iris mid-fall, in a spot with full su~~n~~ The soil should be sandy, mois~~t~~ and well drained. Bulbs should ~~be~~ planted 4 inches deep and 3– inches apart. A winter mulch ~~of~~ leaves or evergreen boughs is re~~c~~ommended. In areas with hot sum~~~mers, dig bulbs out of the groun~~d~~ as soon as the foliage has turne~~d~~ brown in early summer, store in ~~a~~ cool place for 2 months, and repla~~nt~~ in the fall.

Cape Cowslip *(Lachenalia aloides)*

Cape Cowslip has an interesting two-part flower. The short outer segment is yellow, tipped with green; the longer inner segment is yellow, tipped with red. Blooms are 1 inch long and appear in clusters along 12-inch stems in early spring. Basal foliage is 12 inches long and 1 inch wide. The cultivar 'Luteola', pictured here, has lemon-yellow flowers tipped with green; white and lavender cultivars are also available. In some books this species is called *L. tricolor*.

GROWING TIPS

Cape Cowslip is hardy outdoors only in zones 9 and 10, but it may be grown as a pot plant elsewhere. In late summer, plant bulbs 1 inch deep in a light, well-drained, humus-rich soil (or potting medium). Place bulbs in a cool, shady place and keep the soil barely moist. In early winter, move into full sun, increase water, and feed regularly. After flowering, water and fertilize until the leaves start to die down, then cease feeding and reduce watering to keep the soil barely moist until the cycle begins again.

Giant Snowflake *(Leucojum aestivum)*

A member of the amaryllis family, this species is also called Summer Snowflake, although it blooms in mid-spring; the common name distinguishes it from the earlier blooming Spring Snowflake, *Leucojum vernum.* Both have nodding, fragrant white flowers, blooming in loose clusters on a 12- to 18-inch stem. This flower looks like a large Lily-of-the-Valley, except that its foliage is strap shaped. It can be planted in a border or in the flower garden.

GROWING TIPS

Plant Summer Snowflake in full s▮ to partial shade in sandy, rich, we▮ drained soil. Bulbs should ▮ planted in early fall to mid-fall, ▮ inches deep and 4 inches apar▮ Summer Snowflake grows well f▮ many years without decline ar▮ rarely needs dividing.

This plant is closely related to the Summer Snowflake, *Leuco-m aestivum,* but is earlier blooming d smaller in size. The fragrant ite flowers, which have yellow- or een-tipped petals, bloom in early ring along a 6- to 9-inch stem. se Spring Snowflakes in clumps tween shrubs, in rock gardens, or low borders.

GROWING TIPS

Spring Snowflake grows best in full sun to partial shade in sandy, rich, well-drained soil. Plant bulbs in early to mid-fall, 4 inches deep and 3 inches apart. They can be left in place for many years without being disturbed or divided.

Lily *(Lilium)*

Although many lilies flower in summer, there are several that bloom in late spring. These include *L. amabile*, with drooping, 2-inch flowers of orange-red with dark spots on 2-foot stems; Japanese Turk's-Cap Lily, (*L. Hansonii*, pictured here) with fragrant, drooping 1¼-inch flowers of orange-yellow with purple spots on 4–5-foot stems; Turk's-Cap Lily, *L. Martagon*, with drooping, 2-inch flowers of white through pink and purple to almost black on 4- to 6-foot stems; Caucasian Lily, *L. monadelphum*, with fragrant, drooping, 5-inch, golden-yellow flowers on 5-fo stems; and Wood Lily, *L. philade phicum*, with erect, cup-shaped, inch flowers, spotted with orang red, borne on stems 2–3 feet tall.

Growing Tips

Plant lilies in fall, in sun or parti shade and light, rich, perfect drained soil covered with a deep o ganic mulch. The bottom of th bulb should be 3 times as dee below the surface as the bulb high. Fertilize when growth star and keep the soil moist.

Grape-Hyacinth *(Muscari)*

Grape-hyacinths have cone-shaped clusters of drooping, bell-shaped flowers in mid-spring. They combine well with daffodils, tulips, and spring-flowering trees. The flowers are deep blue to purple and look like tiny clusters of grapes. Two popular species, *M. armeniacum* and *M. botryoides,* (called Bluebells or Starch Hyacinth) are similar in appearance. The former grows 4–8 inches tall; *M. botryoides,* pictured here, grows 6–12 inches high, has darker flowers, and foliage that grows closer to the ground.

GROWING TIPS

Grape-hyacinths should be grown in full sun to partial shade in sandy, rich, well-drained soil. Plant them in mid-fall, 3 inches deep and 4 inches apart. They require little attention and rarely need dividing, although you can divide them if you want to increase your stock. The species also freely self-seed. Foliage often appears in the fall; it may turn brown and become rather untidy-looking.

Narcissus *(Narcissus asturiensis)*

The earliest of all daffodils to bloom, this bulb produces plants only 4–5 inches high. The yellow flowers are ½–1 inch long and look like miniature daffodils, blooming one to a stem. The trumpet is longer than the outer petals, which spread or arch backwards. The leaves are linear, 2–4 inches long. Blooming in late winter, this daffodil does best in a rock garden or near the front door where it can be enjoyed as a harbinger of spring. It can also be naturalized in lawns.

GROWING TIPS

Plant *Narcissus asturiensis* in full sun or light shade in light, rich, well drained soil. Excellent drainage in winter is essential. Plant bulbs in mid- to late fall, 4 inches deep and 4 inches apart, and mulch with leaves or evergreen boughs after planting; select the location carefully, because the flowers turn to face the sun. Applying light fertilizer when shoots first appear in spring may increase bloom size. When clumps become crowded every 4 years or so, divide them in late spring, after the leaves ripen.

Petticoat Daffodil (*Narcissus Bulbocodium*) Zones 6–7

The inch-long central cup is flared like a hoop skirt, hence the common name. The surrounding petals are very tiny and often not noticeable. The flowers are usually yellow but may be white; they bloom singly. Plants grow 6–18 inches high and have long leaves. Petticoat (or "Hoop-Petticoat") Daffodil blooms in early spring. Grow it in a rock garden or in the lawn.

GROWING TIPS

The Petticoat Daffodil should be grown in full sun or light shade in light, rich, well-drained soil. Excellent drainage in winter is essential. Plant bulbs in mid- to late fall, about a month before soil becomes cold, 4 inches deep and 4 inches apart, and mulch with leaves or evergreen boughs after planting. The flowers will turn to face the sun, so choose your location with care. Apply fertilizer lightly when shoots first appear in spring. If clumps become crowded, divide in late spring after the foliage turns brown.

Tenby Daffodil (*Narcissus obvallaris*)

This is the famous daffodil of 18th-century English gardens, where it became naturalized. It is a trumpet daffodil, with canary-yellow flowers 1–2½ inches long; single blooms appear on 8- to 12-inch stems. The leaves are linear and 8–12 inches long. The Tenby Daffodil blooms in very early spring.

GROWING TIPS

Plant *Narcissus obvallaris* in full s[un] or light shade in light, rich, we[ll]-drained soil; locate plants with ca[re] as the blooms will face the sun. E[x]-cellent drainage in winter is esse[n]-tial. Plant bulbs in mid- to late fa[ll] 6 inches deep and 6 inches apa[rt]; apply a mulch of leaves or evergre[en] boughs after planting. For larg[e] blooms, you may wish to add a lig[ht] treatment of fertilizer when sho[ots] first appear in spring. When clum[ps] become crowded, divide in l[ate] spring after the foliage turns brow[n].

lso called Trumpet Narcissus, this plant is the true, or orig-al, daffodil, the parent of many rms and cultivars for the garden. e leaves are flat, 12–18 inches ng, usually just reaching the top the flowering stem. The yellow umpet is 2 inches long; it very ten is deeply wavy or slightly nged. The surrounding petals ay be yellow or a different color. blooms singly in early spring.

GROWING TIPS

Plant Common Daffodil in full sun or light shade in light, rich, well-drained soil. Like other *Narcissus*, these flowers will turn to face the sun, so choose their site with care. Excellent drainage in winter is es-sential; some experts recommend setting bulbs on a handful of sand to ensure good drainage. Plant bulbs in mid- to late fall, 6 inches deep and 6–8 inches apart; mulch with leaves or evergreen boughs. Plants will need dividing every few years; divide in late spring after the foliage turns brown.

These flowers are hybrids of *N. cyclamineus,* which has drooping, deep yellow trumpets and petals that flare straight back so that they are parallel with the trumpets. The hybrids have small flowers, ½– 2 inches across, with long, wavy trumpets; the surrounding petals flare backward. There is one flower per 6- to 10-inch stem. Cyclamineus Narcissus bloom in early spring; the best-known varieties are 'Beryl', 'February Gold', 'February Silver', 'Tête-à-Tête', and 'Peeping Tom', pictured here.

GROWING TIPS

Plant Cyclamineus Narcissus hybrids in full sun or light shade light, rich, well-drained soil. Sel the location carefully, because flo ers turn to face the sun. Excelle drainage in winter is essential. Pl bulbs in mid- to late fall, 4 inc deep and 4 inches apart, and mul with leaves or evergreen boug after planting. Apply fertilizer wh shoots first appear in spring. Div in late spring after the foliage tu brown if clumps become crowded

ouble Narcissus *(Narcissus)*

he double-flowered narcissus hybrids and varieties have many ers of petals in the middle of the wer, but they lack a distinct cup trumpet. The central petals are terspersed with smaller petals, en of a different color. These wers bloom in mid- to late ring. They may be white, yellow, a combination of these colors, th 1 or more flowers on each m. The blooms are 2–3 inches de; flowering stems are 14–18 ches high. 'Cheerfulness' is seen re; other popular cultivars are ngkor', 'Ascot', and 'Tahiti'.

GROWING TIPS

Double Narcissus should be grown in full sun or light shade in light, rich, well-drained soil. Excellent drainage in winter is essential: you may wish to set the bulbs on a handful of sand. Plant bulbs in mid- to late fall, 6 inches deep and 6–8 inches apart, and mulch with leaves or evergreen boughs after planting. Apply fertilizer when shoots first appear in spring to encourage larger blooms. Clumps may become crowded after a few years; divide in late spring after the foliage turns brown.

Jonquilla Narcissus (*Narcissus*)

The Jonquilla Narcissus group includes hybrids of *N. Jonquilla*, the Common Jonquil, which has clusters of 1-inch, fragrant yellow flowers on an 18-inch stem. The hybrids also bloom in clusters of flowers that have small cups and heavy fragrance. The flowers are ½–1 inch long; stems are 12 inches long. Blooms may have yellow, pink, red, or orange cups and yellow or white petals. Foliage is reedlike and dark green. The plants bloom in mid-spring. The variety 'Lemon Tarts' is pictured here.

GROWING TIPS

Plant Jonquilla Narcissus in full s or light shade; in choosing a sp remember that the blooms will to to face the sun. Soil should be lig rich, and well drained; excelle drainage is particularly important winter. Bulbs should be planted mid- to late fall, 6 inches deep a 6–8 inches apart; mulch with lea or evergreen boughs after plantir For larger blooms, apply fertili lightly when shoots first appear spring. In late spring, after the liage turns brown, you can div clumps if they are crowded.

arge-cupped Narcissus hybrids ⌐ include flowers whose cup meaⁱres more than a third but less than ₑ total length of the surrounding ⁻tals. The cup may be yellow, ʰite, pink, or red; the surrounding segments are yellow or white. ₒwers are 4½ inches wide and ₒom singly on a 14- to 20-inch ⁻em. 'Flower Record' is seen here; ʰer popular kinds are 'Aranjuez', ⁾elibes', 'Ice Follies', 'Prof. Einⁱein', 'Roulette', and 'Rushlight'. ʰey bloom in early spring to midⁱring, usually after the Trumpet ᵃrcissus group.

GROWING TIPS

These bulbs need full sun or light shade and light, rich, well-drained soil. Excellent drainage in winter is essential. Plant bulbs in mid- to late fall, 6 inches deep and 6–8 inches apart; after planting, apply a mulch of leaves or evergreen boughs. A light treatment of fertilizer, applied when shoots first appear in spring, may increase bloom size. When clumps become crowded, divide in late spring after the foliage turns brown.

Poeticus Narcissus *(Narcissus)*

The flowers in this class include the wild and garden forms of *N. poeticus*, the Poet's Narcissus. The species is distinctive; its fragrant, 1-inch flowers have large, curved white petals and very short yellow cups with red margins. The Poeticus Narcissus hybrids are similar, with glistening white petals and centers that are almost flat. The central "eye" may be yellow with a red margin, red, or even green. All hybrids are fragrant and bloom singly; they grow to 18 inches tall and appear in mid-spring to late spring. The cultivar 'Actaea' is seen here.

GROWING TIPS

These delicate narcissus do best in full sun; the blossoms will all face the sun, so choose a location with care. Soil should be light, rich, and well drained; excellent drainage especially important in winter. Plant bulbs in mid-fall to late fall, 6 inches deep and 6–8 inches apart. Mulch with leaves or evergreen boughs after planting. A light fertilizer may be applied when shoots first appear in spring for larger blooms. Divide in late spring after the foliage turns brown if clumps become crowded.

mall-cupped Narcissus are characterized by a cup that measures o more than a third the length of he surrounding petals. These flowers grow to 3 inches wide—slightly maller than members of the Largeupped class types—and bloom sinly. The flowering stems grow to 15 nches high. Small-cupped hybrids ome in various colors—with yelow, white, pink, or red cups surounded by yellow or white. Birma', pictured here, and 'Barrett Browning' are well-known cultiars. All bloom in early spring.

GROWING TIPS

Select a sunny spot with light, rich, well-drained soil. The blooms, when they appear, will face the sun, so plant your bulbs accordingly. Excellent drainage in winter is essential to prevent bulb rot. Plant bulbs in mid-fall to late fall, 6 inches deep and 6–8 inches apart. Mulch with leaves or evergreen boughs after planting. You may wish to apply fertilizer when shoots first appear in spring to encourage larger blossoms. When clumps become crowded, divide in late spring after the foliage turns brown.

Split-corona Narcissus *(Narcissus)*

Sometimes called Butterfly Daffodils, these hybrids have the cup split for at least a third of its length, with the split portions spreading back against the petals. Split-corona Narcissus often resemble daffodils and often look like Double Narcissus hybrids. The flowers are 3 inches across and bloom singly; flowering stems grow 16–20 inches high. They bloom in mid-spring to late spring. 'Egard', seen here, and 'Palmares' are good garden cultivars. The cup can be white, yellow, orange, or pink; the petals are white or yellow.

GROWING TIPS

Plant Split-corona Narcissus in full sun or light shade in light, rich, well-drained soil. Excellent drainage in winter is essential. Bulbs should be planted in mid-fall to late fall, 6 inches deep and 6–8 inches apart; mulch with leaves or evergreen boughs after planting. For larger blooms, apply fertilizer when shoots first appear in spring. Divide in late spring after the foliage turns brown when clumps become crowded, usually about every fourth year.

Tazetta Narcissus *(Narcissus)*

In this class are varieties and hybrids of *Narcissus Tazetta*, including hybrids once known as "Poetaz." The species has flat leaves, 8 inches long and ¾ inch wide, and clusters of fragrant, 1-inch flowers that are often white. The popular horticultural forms grow 12–18 inches high, with flowers ½–1¼ inches wide; these include 'Canary Bird', 'Cragford' (seen here), 'Geranium', 'Paper-white', and 'Soleil d'Or'. The last two are tender and often forced indoors. All are fragrant and bloom in clusters in late spring.

GROWING TIPS

Plant Tazetta Narcissus in full sun. Select the location carefully, for the flowers turn to face the sun. Soil should be light, rich, and well drained, with excellent drainage in winter. Plant bulbs in mid- to late fall, 6 inches deep and 6–8 inches apart, and mulch with leaves or evergreen boughs after planting. Divide every 4 years in late spring after the foliage turns brown. To force bulbs in pebbles and water, allow roots to develop well before bringing plants to light. A cool room will give best results.

Triandrus Narcissus *(Narcissus)*

The pure white blooms of *Narcissus triandrus* are 1–1½ inches wide with a short cup. The hybrids and varieties of this species that make up this class are graceful plants, with drooping clusters of flowers with short cups and recurving petals. Triandrus Narcissus bloom in mid-spring to late spring. 'Hawera', one popular cultivar, is 8 inches high and has yellow flowers; 'Thalia', seen here, grows to 16 inches and has white flowers. Other cultivars are all-yellow, all-white, or with yellow cups and white petals.

GROWING TIPS

Plant Triandrus Narcissus hybrids in full sun or light shade; remember that the blooms will face the sun when they appear. Light, rich, well-drained soil is important, and excellent drainage in winter is essential to prevent waterlogging and rot. Plant bulbs in mid-fall to late fall, 6 inches deep and 6–8 inches apart; apply a mulch of leaves or evergreen boughs after planting. Every few years, clumps will become crowded; divide in late spring, after the foliage turns brown.

These hybrids include the largest of the daffodils, which have a rumpet as long as or longer than the surrounding petals. Trumpet Narcissus bloom singly; the flowers may be all-white, all-yellow, or have a yellow trumpet surrounded by white petals. The blooms are 3–4 inches wide and appear on 16- to 20-inch stems in early spring to mid-spring. Popular cultivars are 'Foresight', 'King Alfred', 'Mount Hood', and 'Unsurpassable' (pictured here).

GROWING TIPS

Trumpet Narcissus should be grown in full sun or light shade; the blooms will face the sun, so select your site accordingly. They require light, rich, well-drained soil, and must have excellent drainage in winter. Plant bulbs in mid-fall to late fall, 6 inches deep and 6–8 inches apart; mulch with leaves or evergreen boughs after planting. Apply fertilizer when shoots appear in spring for larger blooms. Divide every few years, when bulbs become crowded; late spring, after the foliage turns brown, is the best time.

Nectaroscordum *(Nectaroscordum)*

There are two species in this little-known genus, both of which bear clusters of drooping flowers at the tops of 4-foot stems. *N. siculum* has greenish-white flowers tinged with purple and pink. Seen here is *N. bulgaricum*, which is sometimes regarded as a subspecies of *N. siculum*. It is similar in appearance but slightly more slender. Foliage in both is narrow and lance shaped and up to 2 feet long. Flowers appear in early spring.

GROWING TIPS

Plant nectaroscordum in full sun in any rich, well-drained garden soil. They like to be watered well during the growing season. Set them into the ground in mid-fall, 6 inches deep and 12 inches apart. Apply winter protection in the northern limits of their hardiness.

ar-of-Bethlehem *(Ornithogalum nutans)* Zone 6

Two or more species share the common name Star-of-Bethlehem, although the plants are quite different in appearance. The species shown here, *O. nutans*, has a flowering stem 8–12 inches high that bears from 3 to 12 nodding blooms with backward-sweeping petals. Each fragrant flower is 2 inches wide, white inside and green on the outside. Plants bloom in mid-spring. Leaves are pale green and 12–18 inches long. This species grows well in the woodland garden.

GROWING TIPS

Plant Star-of-Bethlehem in full sun to partial shade in any well-drained garden soil. It is easy to grow and increases very rapidly. Plant bulbs in mid-fall, 4 inches deep and 4 inches apart. Divide frequently, every 2 to 3 years, as soon as the clumps become crowded.

Star-of-Bethlehem *(Ornithogalum umbellatum)*

Sharing a common name with its relative, *Ornithogalum nutans,* this species is a low-growing bulb with flowering stems growing 6–8 inches tall. Flowers bloom in mid-spring, 12–20 in a cluster. The individual blooms are 1 inch across, white, striped in green on the outsides of the petals; they open flat. Leaves grow in grassy clumps as high as the flower stems and are veined or spotted with white. This Star-of-Bethlehem is best used in the wild garden.

GROWING TIPS

Plant this Star-of-Bethlehem in mid-fall, setting bulbs 4 inches deep and 4 inches apart. Locate bulbs in full sun or partial shade in any well-drained soil. The species tolerates poor, dry soil and increases rapidly. Divide every 2 or 3 years as soon as the clumps become crowded. It can be used as a cut flower, but the blooms close up at night.

Violet Wood Sorrel *(Oxalis violacea)*

A pretty little plant suitable for the rock garden or the wild garden, Violet Wood Sorrel grows -10 inches high. The three-part leaves resemble those of clover and d up at night. The clusters of ¾-ch flowers bloom on stalks that e from the ground. Blooms are ually rose to purple but may rarely pale pinkish white; they appear in e spring.

GROWING TIPS
Plant Violet Wood Sorrel in partial shade in rich, acid, well-drained soil. Plant the bulbs in early fall to mid-fall; they should be 4 inches deep and 4 inches apart. They naturalize easily and can be left in place many years without dividing.

Striped Squill *(Puschkinia scilloides)*

From a distance, Striped Squill looks like a pale blue flower, but its blooms are actually white with a fine, light blue stripe. They bloom in dense clusters, 4–6 inches high, in early spring; strap-shaped basal leaves surround the flowers. Striped Squill is best grown in a naturalized garden and combines well with Siberian Squill and Glory-of-the-Snow, which bloom at the same time in spring.

GROWING TIPS

Plant Striped Squill in early fa setting the bulbs 3 inches deep a 3 inches apart. They may be plant in full sun or partial shade and well under deciduous trees, whi do not leaf out until after the bu bloom. Soil should be sandy, ferti and well drained. Striped Squ self-sows readily, and large colon will quickly form.

Scillas, also known as squill, are easy to grow and work well as carpet plants for beds of May tulips. Siberian Squill, *S. siberica,* grows 4– inches high and bears clusters of to 5 flowers on wiry stems. The blooms are deep blue to purple and appear in very early spring with Striped Squill and Glory-of-the Snow. Excellent for the rock garden, can also be combined with *S. Tuergeniana* (pictured), which is similar in appearance but grows 5 inches high and has larger flowers of white or pale blue.

GROWING TIPS

Plant scillas in full sun or partial shade in rich, sandy, well-drained soil. Plant bulbs in fall, 2–3 inches deep and 3 inches apart. They self-sow freely and quickly form large clumps. Once planted, they should not be disturbed and rarely need to be divided.

Turkish Tulip *(Tulipa acuminata)*

The spidery-looking Turkish Tulip provides a touch of the unusual to the tulip bed. It has 3- to 4-inch flowers long, pointed, and somewhat twisted petals. The stems grow 12–18 inches; the leaves are narrow and irregularly curving. Turkish Tulip blooms in mid- to late spring.

GROWING TIPS

Plant Turkish Tulips in full sun temperate regions; in hot areas, pa tial shade is preferred, and it w extend the blooming period of th late-flowering variety. Soil shoul be sandy, well drained, and rich. mid-fall, set bulbs 4–6 inches dee and 6 inches apart. Protect from r dents with a screen of chicken wi secured on top of the beds. Fertili when shoots emerge in spring. Yc can dig up and divide bulbs every or 3 years if blooms become smalle some gardeners prefer to replac bulbs every few years.

This tulip's fragrant, dainty blooms are 2 inches long, ointed, and white or yellow, with oad red stripes on the outside, ith reddish purple at the base of e petals. Flowering stems are 9– 5 inches tall over narrow foliage. his is a good tulip for cutting. The riety *chrysantha*, seen here, has llow petals striped on the outside red; it lacks the purple base on e petals. Both bloom in mid- to te spring.

GROWING TIPS

Plant tulips in sandy, rich, well-drained soil in full sun; partial shade is preferred in hot areas and will extend the blooming period of late-flowering kinds. In mid-fall, set bulbs 4–6 inches deep and 6 inches apart; protect them from rodents with a screen of chicken wire secured on top of the beds. Fertilize when shoots emerge in spring. If blooms become smaller, dig bulbs and divide every 2 to 3 years, or replace them altogether. Division should be performed after the foliage has withered.

Tulip *(Tulipa Kolpakowskiana)*

This low-growing tulip, which lacks a real common name, has flowering stems 6 inches long. Flowers are 2 inches long with spreading, pointed petals; these are yellow on the inside and red on the outside. One or 2 flowers may appear on each stem. Leaves are blue-green, narrow, and pointed, 6–8 inches long. *Tulipa Kolpakowskiana* blooms in early spring.

GROWING TIPS

Tulips grow well in full sun, b[…] partial shade is preferred in h[…] areas. Soil should be sandy, we[…] drained, and rich. In mid-fall, s[…] bulbs 4–6 inches deep and 4 inch[…] apart. Protect from rodents with […] screen of chicken wire secured o[…] top of the beds. Fertilize whe[…] shoots emerge in spring. If bloom[…] become smaller, dig bulbs and d[…] vide every 2–3 years, or repla[…] them altogether.

ulip *(Tulipa praestans)*

A medium-sized tulip, this species grows to 12 inches tall.
has narrow, tapering leaves and
d, single blooms to 2 inches long.
he cultivar 'Fusilier' has 4 to 6
owers per stem. Bloom time is
rly spring.

GROWING TIPS

Tulips do best in full sun, except in
hot areas, where partial shade is preferred. Plant bulbs in mid-fall, 4–6
inches deep and 6 inches apart. Secure a screen of chicken wire on top
of the beds to protect the bulbs from
rodents. Soil should be sandy, well
drained, and rich. Fertilize when
shoots emerge in spring. After 2
to 3 years, blooms may become
smaller; you may dig the bulbs and
divide them in midsummer, after
foliage has withered; some gardeners
prefer to replace the bulbs with new
ones.

Tulip *(Tulipa pulchella)*

A low-growing species, this tulip grows just 4–6 inches high. Its flowers are cup-shaped and 1½ inches long; they open flat to reveal the yellow center. Petals may be red, purple, violet, or white. Each plant bears 2 to 3 narrow, pointed, smooth leaves. *Tulipa pulchella* blooms in early spring.

GROWING TIPS

Tulips prefer full sun, except in ho areas, where partial shade suits ther best. They need sandy, well drained, rich soil. Plant bulbs i mid-fall, 4–6 inches deep and inches apart. Protect bulbs from ro dents with a screen of chicken wir secured on top of the beds. Whe shoots emerge in spring, apply ligh fertilizer. Dig and divide bulb every 2 to 3 years if blooms becom smaller.

The cup-shaped, fragrant, pale lilac petals of this species have large yellow base. *Tulipa saxatilis* ten blooms in clusters of 2 to 3; ch flower is 2 inches across, and e flowering stems are 12 inches gh. Leaves are flat and shiny een. Bloom time is mid-spring.

GROWING TIPS

ulips grow well in full sun but ey will tolerate partial shade; par-al shade is preferred in hot areas nd will extend the blooming pe-riod. Plant bulbs in mid-fall in sandy, rich, well-drained soil; set 4 to 6 inches deep and 6 inches apart. Secure a screen of chicken wire on top of the beds to protect the bulbs from rodents. Feed with a light application of fertilizer when shoots emerge in spring. Dig bulbs and divide them every 2 to 3 years if blooms become smaller, or replace them altogether. *T. saxatilis* requires less winter cold than most other tulip species.

Tulip *(Tulipa turkestanica)*

A vigorous species, *Tulipa turkestanica* grows 8–12 inches high and has clusters of up to 8 flowers per stem. Each star-shaped white flower is 1¼ inches long and has an orange-yellow base. Leaves are lance shaped. The plant blooms in early spring.

Growing Tips

Tulips like full sun, except in ho areas, where partial shade is pre ferred. Set bulbs in mid-fall, 4– inches deep and 6 inches apart, i sandy, rich, well-drained soil. Use screen of chicken wire on top of th beds to keep mice and chipmunk away. Fertilize when shoots emerg in spring. If blooms becom smaller, dig bulbs and divide ther every 2 to 3 years, or replace ther altogether. Division should tak place after the foliage has withered in midsummer.

Cottage Tulip (*Tulipa*)

A favorite in old English cottage gardens, these late-blooming, egg-shaped, 4-inch tulips have pointed or rounded petals. The flexible flowering stems grow up to 36 inches long. This group includes some multiflowering forms such as 'Georgette' and 'Orange Bouquet' and the green-feathered *viridiflora* types. Other popular cultivars, which have no blue or purple forms, are 'Golden Harvest' and pinkish-yellow 'Smiling Queen'; seen here is 'Rosy Wings'. Cottage Tulips are sometimes called Single Late Tulips.

GROWING TIPS

Plant tulips in full sun to partial shade; partial shade is preferred in hot areas and will extend the blooming period. Set the bulbs in late fall, 6 inches deep and 6–8 inches apart, in rich, sandy, well-drained soil. Protect them from rodents with a screen of chicken wire secured on top of the beds. Apply a light dressing of fertilizer when shoots emerge in spring. Replace the bulbs when the flowers start to grow small. In zones 8–10, bulbs should be chilled at 40° F for 2 to 3 weeks before planting.

Darwin Tulip (*Tulipa*)

The hybrids in the class of Darwin Tulips are among the most popular. They bear cup-shaped flowers, 3–4 inches deep, on erect stems up to 30 inches high, and are found in a very wide range of colors, from white to purple-black. Some well-known cultivars are 'Blue Amiable', 'Golden Age', and the almost black 'Queen of the Night'. The white 'Duke of Wellington' is pictured here. Darwin Tulips bloom in late spring; they are often combined with Cottage Tulips under the heading Single Late Tulips.

Growing Tips

Tulips like full sun, but partial shade is preferred in hot areas and will extend the blooming period. Set the bulbs in late fall, 6 inches deep and 6–8 inches apart, in rich, sandy, well-drained soil. Protect bulbs from rodents with a screen of chicken wire secured on top of the beds. Apply a light dressing of fertilizer when shoots emerge in spring. Replace the bulbs when the flowers start to grow small. In zones 8–10, chill bulbs for 2–3 weeks at 40° F before planting.

Darwin Hybrid Tulip *(Tulipa)*

Produced chiefly by crossing Darwin Tulips with *T. Fosteriana*, members of the class have large, oval to egg-shaped flowers with a square base. They are among the largest tulips, up to 4 inches long, and bloom on erect stems up to 30 inches high. Colors range from scarlet through deep yellow. Most popular varieties are red 'Holland's Glory', 'Gudoshnik', and the 'Apeldoorn' and 'Oxford' varieties of gold and red; 'Oxford' is pictured here. All bloom in mid-spring before the Darwins.

GROWING TIPS

Plant tulips in full sun to partial shade; partial shade is preferred in hot areas and will extend the blooming period. Set the bulbs in late fall, 6 inches deep and 6–8 inches apart; soil should be sandy, well drained, and rich. Protect from rodents with a screen of chicken wire secured on top of the beds. Fertilize when shoots emerge in spring. Replace the bulbs when the flowers start to grow small. In zones 8–10, chill bulbs for 2 to 3 weeks at 40° F before planting.

Double Early Tulip *(Tulipa)*

The many-petaled, 4-inch flowers of the hybrids in this class are similar to a peony's, and they last longer than single tulips, both in the garden and as a cut flower. Double Early Tulips also force well. Stems are sturdy and 6–12 inches long. Flower color is mainly red, yellow, orange, or white. Popular cultivars are the red and orange 'Fringed Beauty' (seen here) and 'Orange Nassau'. They bloom in early spring, in almost any weather.

GROWING TIPS

Plant tulips in full sun to partial shade; partial shade is preferred hot areas. Set bulbs in late fall, inches deep and 6–8 inches apart in sandy, rich, well-drained soil. Use a screen of chicken wire, secured on top of the beds, to keep rodents away. Fertilize when shoots emerge in spring. Replace the bulbs when the flowers start to grow small. In zones 8–10, chill bulbs for 2 to 3 weeks at 40° F before planting.

ouble Late Tulip *(Tulipa)*

nown as "Peony-flowered" tulips, the hybrids in this class ave many petals and are long-lasting in the garden or as a cut flower. opular cultivars are the white 'Mount Tacoma' (seen here), and the d 'May Wonder'. Flowers are 6 iches wide and bloom in late oring on 18- to 22-inch stems.

GROWING TIPS

Tulips like full sun in temperate areas, but require partial shade in hot regions; partial shade also extends the blooming period. Plant bulbs in late fall, 6 inches deep and 6–8 inches apart; they need sandy, well-drained, rich soil. Protect bulbs from rodents with a screen of chicken wire secured on top of the beds. Fertilize lightly when shoots emerge in spring, and replace the bulbs when the flowers start to grow small. In zones 8–10, chill bulbs for 2–3 weeks at 40° F before planting. Not resistant to wind or rain.

Fosteriana Tulip (*Tulipa*)

Varieties and hybrids of *T. Fosteriana*, members of this class of tulips bear 4-inch-long flowers that bloom in early spring on 8- to 20-inch stems. The 'Emperor' forms with varieties in white, yellow, gold, orange, and red, and are very popular. The cultivar 'Purissima' is pictured here. The foliage of these tulips is sometimes mottled or striped, as it is in the species.

GROWING TIPS

Tulips should be grown in full su to partial shade; partial shade is pr ferred in hot areas. Plant bulbs sandy, rich, well-drained soil; s them in late fall, 6 inches deep ar 6–8 inches apart. A chicken-wi screen on top of the beds will pr tect bulbs from the incursions chipmunks and mice. When shoo emerge in spring, apply a ligh dressing of fertilizer. Replace th bulbs when the flowers start to gro small, usually after a few years. I zones 8–10, chill bulbs at 40° F fo 2 to 3 weeks before planting.

This class of hybrids is made up of descendants of *Tulipa Greigii*. The species grows 6–10 inches high and has broad, dark, wavy-margined, distinctly mottled or striped foliage. The flowers are 3 inches long, orange-red with a dark base, yellow-margined, and slightly pointed. The hybrids grow 7–14 inches tall and bear similar flowers in mid- to late spring; most are in the red, yellow, and orange range. 'Red Riding Hood' is one of the best-known cultivars, along with the yellow and red 'Cape Cod' (seen here) and 'Flaming Star'.

GROWING TIPS

Tulips should have full sun except in hot regions, where partial shade is preferred and extends the blooming period. Plant bulbs in late fall, 6 inches deep and 6 inches apart, in rich, sandy, well-drained soil. Use a screen of chicken wire secured on top of the beds to keep mice and chipmunks away. Apply fertilizer when shoots emerge in spring. Replace the bulbs when the flowers start to grow small, usually in 2 or 3 years. In zones 8–10, chill bulbs for 2 to 3 weeks at 40° F before planting.

Kaufmanniana Tulip *(Tulipa)* Zone

Good for the rock garden, the tulips in this class bloom in very early spring. They are derived from the Water Lily Tulip *(Tulipa Kaufmanniana)*, which has 3-inch, spreading white or pale yellow flowers with a red-marked yellow center. Flower stems are 5–10 inches high. The species may self-sow and form colonies. The hybrids and varieties grow 4–8 inches high, with similar flowers 3½ inches across. Popular cultivars are the gold 'Giuseppe Verdi'; the white 'Honorose'; 'Johann Strauss', which is white and red; and the orange 'Shakespeare'.

GROWING TIPS

Tulips like full sun, but part shade is preferred in hot areas. Pla bulbs in late fall, 6 inches deep a 4 inches apart, in rich, sandy, we drained soil. Protect them from r dents with a screen of chicken wi secured on top of the beds. Apply light dressing of fertilizer wh shoots emerge in spring. The Kau manniana hybrids are longer lasti than other tulips, needing to be placed less often. In zones 8–1 chill bulbs for 2 to 3 weeks at 40° before planting.

98 BULBS FOR SPRING

ily-flowered Tulip *(Tulipa)*

t is easy to see where this class of tulips got its name—the flowers ve long, pointed petals that curve tward at the tips. The flowers are -4 inches long and bloom in late ring on 2-foot stems. Well- own cultivars are the pink-and- ite 'Ballade', seen here; the yel- w 'West Point'; 'Queen of Sheba', ich is orange; and the purple aytime'. All make excellent cut wers.

GROWING TIPS

Plant tulips in full sun except in hot areas, where partial shade is preferred and will extend the blooming period. Set bulbs in late fall, 6 inches deep and 6–8 inches apart, in sandy, rich, well-drained soil. Protect from rodents with a screen of chicken wire secured on top of the beds. Apply a light fertilizer when shoots emerge in spring. Replace the bulbs when the flowers start to grow small, usually every 2 to 3 years. In zones 8–10, chill bulbs for 2 to 3 weeks at 40° F before planting.

Parrot Tulip *(Tulipa)*

The flowers grouped in the Parrot Tulip class are "sports," or chance mutations, of other tulips. The blooms are 6–7 inches across, with twisted fringed, cut, or feathered petals, often with green markings. The flowers are borne on weak stems, to 24 inches high. Parrot Tulips bloom in late spring. Popular varieties include 'Blue Parrot'; the yellow-and-red-striped 'Flaming Parrot' (pictured here); 'Karel Doorman', a red cultivar; the white-and-red or yellow-and-red 'Texas'; and 'Yellow Parrot'.

GROWING TIPS

Plant tulips in full sun to part shade in sandy, rich, well-drain soil. Partial shade is preferred in h areas and will extend the bloomi period. Set bulbs in late fall, inches deep and 6–8 inches apa Protect from rodents with a scre of chicken wire secured on top of t beds. When shoots emerge spring, apply a light dressing of f tilizer. Replace the bulbs when t flowers start to grow small, usua after a few years. In zones 8–1 chill bulbs for 2 to 3 weeks at 40° before planting.

ingle Early Tulip *(Tulipa)*

imilar in appearance to the Cottage or Darwin tulips, with egg-aped, 2- to 4-inch flowers, Single arly Tulips are shorter than the ter-flowering tulips, growing 10–5 inches high. Flowers are gen-ally red, yellow, or white; many e fragrant. Blooming in early ring, these tulips are also good for rcing. The yellow 'Bellona', pic-red here, is a popular variety. Sin-e Early Tulips are more weather-sistant than most of the later ooming varieties.

GROWING TIPS

Tulips like full sun to partial shade; in hot areas, partial shade is preferred. Plant bulbs in late fall, 6 inches deep and 6 inches apart, in rich, sandy, well-drained soil. Protect them from rodents with a screen of chicken wire on top of the beds. Fertilize when shoots emerge in spring. Replace the bulbs when the flowers start to grow small. Before planting in zones 8–10, chill bulbs for 2 to 3 weeks at 40° F.

Triumph Tulip *(Tulipa)*

Members of this class are primarily crosses between the Single Early Tulips and later-flowering forms; they bloom in midspring between the two. Flowers are 2–4 inches long, single, and egg-shaped; they bloom on 20-inch stems. Vigorous and robust, Triumph Tulips are good for forcing and cutting. Among popular cultivars are the orange-and-red 'Kees Nelis' and the pink-and-white-striped 'Garden Party', shown here.

GROWING TIPS

Tulips like full sun, but partial shade is preferred in hot areas. Plant the bulbs in late fall in rich, sandy, well-drained soil; set them 6 inches deep and 6–8 inches apart. A screen of chicken wire secured on top of the beds will help protect them from rodents. When shoots emerge in spring, apply a light dressing of fertilizer. Replace the bulbs when the flowers start to grow small. In zones 8–10, chill bulbs for 2 to 3 weeks at 40° F before planting.

nicorn Root *(Veltheimia viridifolia)*

Unicorn Root is characterized by foliage so shiny it looks as though it were varnished. Its leaves e 12 inches long and 3 inches ide, with wavy margins. The pink yellow flowers with green tips are bular and drooping; they bloom early spring in spikes at the ends f 2-foot stems.

GROWING TIPS

lant Unicorn Root outdoors in partal shade and rich, well-drained soil hat is moist during winter and spring and dry in summer. This species can be grown anywhere as a container plant, and is hardy outdoors in zones 9 and 10. To grow in pots, pot up bulbs in early fall, with one-third of the bulb above the soil level, and place the pots indoors in a cool room or greenhouse. Water sparingly to keep the soil barely moist. When leaves appear in late winter, increase watering. When leaves die down in summer, reduce watering, keeping the soil barely moist, and repeat the cycle. Do not repot every year.

Atamasco Lily *(Zephyranthes Atamasco)*

The funnel-shaped, 6-petaled flowers of this species (also called Fairy Lily) bloom in early spring on 12-inch stems. The blooms are 3 inches long and pure white or white tinted with pale purple. The leaves are 12 inches long and very narrow.

GROWING TIPS

Atamasco Lily requires full sun and rich, well-drained soil. Plant bulbs in fall, 1–2 inches deep and 3 inches apart; keep soil moist during the growing season and dry in summer.

In zone 7, mulch with evergree boughs, leaves, or straw durin winter. In areas colder than zone 7 lift the bulbs in fall after the firs frost and store them indoors durin the winter; do not allow bulbs t dry out during storage. Atamasc Lily can also be grown in containers Keep soil constantly moist durin the growing period; then allow it t dry out, so that it is barely mois during the late summer and fall until growth restarts.

APPENDICES

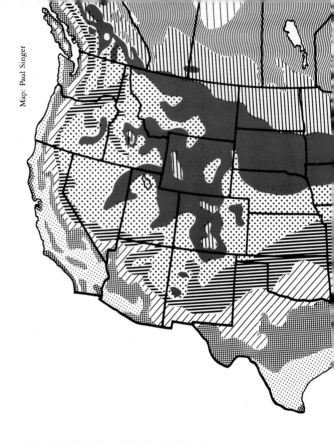

HARDINESS ZONE MAP

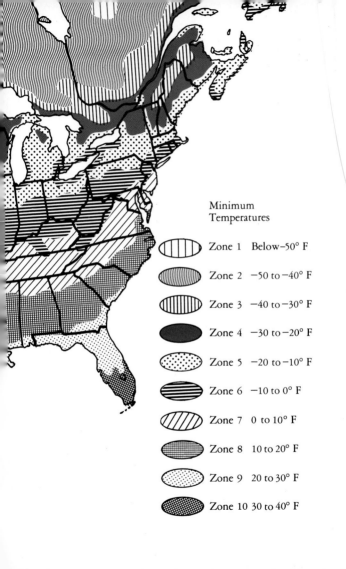

Minimum
Temperatures

Zone 1   Below –50° F

Zone 2   –50 to –40° F

Zone 3   –40 to –30° F

Zone 4   –30 to –20° F

Zone 5   –20 to –10° F

Zone 6   –10 to 0° F

Zone 7   0 to 10° F

Zone 8   10 to 20° F

Zone 9   20 to 30° F

Zone 10 30 to 40° F

GARDEN PESTS AND DISEASES

PLANT PESTS and diseases are a fact of life for a gardener. Therefore, it is helpful to become familiar with common pests and diseases in your area and to learn how to control them.

Symptoms of Plant Problems

Because the same general symptoms are associated with many diseases and pests, some experience is needed to determine their causes.

Diseases

Both fungi and bacteria are responsible for a variety of diseases ranging from leaf spots and wilts to root rot, but bacterial diseases usually make the affected plant tissues appear wetter than fungi do. Diseases caused by viruses and mycoplasma, often transmitted by aphids and leafhoppers, display such symptoms as mottled yellow or deformed leaves and stunted or twisted growth.

Insect Pests

Numerous insects attack plants. Sap-sucking insects—including aphids, leafhoppers, and scale insects—suck plant juices. The affected plant becomes yellow, stunted, and misshapen. Aphids and scale insects produce honeydew, a sticky substance that attracts ants and sooty mold fungus growth. Other pests with rasping-sucking mouthparts, such as thrips and spider mites, scrape plant tissue and then suck the juices that well up in the injured areas.

Leaf-chewers, namely beetles, consume plant leaves, whole or in part. Borers tunnel into shoots and stems, and their young larvae consume plant tissue, weakening the plant. Some insects, such as various grubs and maggots, feed on roots, weakening or killing the plant.

Nematodes

Microscopic roundworms called nematodes are other pests that attack roots and cause stunting and poor plant growth. Some kinds of nematodes produce galls on roots, while others produce them on leaves.

Environmental Stresses

Some types of plant illness result from environment-related stress, such as severe wind, drought, flooding, or extreme cold. Other problems are caused by salt toxicity, rodents, birds, nutritional deficiencies or excesses, pesticides, or damage from lawn mowers. Many of these injuries are avoidable if you take proper precautions.

Controlling Plant Problems

Purchase bulbs that are firm and robust, not shriveled and spongy, then make sure you store them properly once you get them home. If you are buying plants, check the leaves and stems for dead areas or off-color and stunted tissue. If possible, buy disease-resistant varieties. Before you plant your bulbs, prepare the soil properly.

Routine Preventives

By cultivating the soil routinely you will expose insects and disease-causing organisms to the sun and thus lessen their chances of surviving in your garden. In the fall, be sure to destroy infested or diseased plants, remove dead leaves and flowers, and clean up plant debris. Do not add diseased or infested material to the compost pile. Spray plants with water from time to time to dislodge insect pests and remove suffocating dust. Pick off the larger insects by hand. To discourage fungal leaf spots and blights, always water plants in the morning and allow the leaves to dry off before nightfall. For the same reason, provide adequate air circulation around leaves and stems by spacing plants properly.

Weeds provide a home for insects and diseases, so pull them up or use herbicides. But do not apply herbicides, including "weed-and-feed" lawn preparations, too close to flower beds. Herbicide injury may cause leaves to become elongated, straplike, or downward-cupping. Spray weed-killers when there is little air movement, but not on a very hot, dry day.

Insecticides and Fungicides

To protect plant tissue from injury due to insects and diseases, a number of insecticides and fungicides are available. However, few products control diseases due to bacteria, viruses, and mycoplasma. Pesticides are usually either "protectant" or "systemic" in nature. Protectants keep uninfected foliage safe from insects or disease organisms, while systemics move through the plant and provide some therapeutic or eradicant action as well as protection. Botanical insecticides such as pyrethrum and rotenone have a shorter residual effect on pests, but are considered less toxic and generally safer for the user and the environment than inorganic chemical insecticides. Biological control through the use of organisms like *Bacillus thuringiensis* (a bacterium toxic to moth and butterfly larvae) is effective and safe.

Recommended pesticides may vary to some extent from region to region. Consult your local Cooperative Extension Service or plant professional regarding the appropriate material to use. Always check the pesticide label to be sure that it is registered for use on the pest and plant with which you are dealing. Follow the label concerning safety precautions, dosage, and frequency of application.

GLOSSARY

Acid soil
Soil with a pH value of less than 7.

Alkaline soil
Soil with a pH value of more than 7.

Alternate
Of leaves, arranged singly along a twig or shoot, and not in whorls or opposite pairs.

Annual
A plant whose entire life span, from sprouting to flowering and producing seeds, is encompassed in a single growing season. Annuals survive cold or dry seasons as dormant seeds. See also Biennial and Perennial.

Axil
The angle formed by a petiole and the stem from which it grows.

Axis
The central stalk of a compound leaf or flower cluster; also, the main stem of a plant.

Basal leaf
A leaf at the base of a stem.

Berry
A fleshy fruit containing one or more seeds, developed from a single ovary.

Biennial
A plant whose life span extends to two growing seasons; a biennial plant sprouts in the first growing season; in the second, it flowers, produces seeds or fruit, and dies.

Blade
The broad, flat part of a leaf.

Bract
A modified and often scalelike leaf, usually located at the base of a flower, a fruit, or a cluster of flowers or fruits.

Bristle
A stiff, short hair on a stem or leaf.

Bud
A young and undeveloped shoot, usually covered tightly with scales, that may develop into a leafy shoot or a flower.

Bulb
A short, vertical, underground stem, with a swollen portion consisting mostly of fleshy, food-storing leaf bases.

Bulbil
A small bulblike structure, usually borne among the flowers or in the axil of a leaf, never at ground level like a true bulb.

Bulblet
A small bulb produced at the periphery of a larger bulb.

Calyx
Collectively, the sepals of a flower.

Clasping
Surrounding or partly surrounding the stem, as in the base of the leaves of certain plants.

Compound leaf
A leaf made up of two or more leaflets.

Corm
A solid, vertical, underground stem, resembling a bulb, with a bud on top and often with a membranous coat of dried leaf bases.

Cormel
A small corm that is produced by and develops alongside of its parent corm. Also called a "cormlet."

Corolla
Collectively, the petals of a flower.

Corona
A crownlike structure borne at the center of the corolla of some flowers, such as daffodils.

Crest
A ridge or appendage on petals, flower clusters, or leaves.

Cross-pollination
The transfer of pollen from the flower of one plant to the pistil of another plant.

Crown
The base of a plant stem, just above the roots and usually at soil level. In herbaceous perennials, overwintering buds are located in the crown.

Cultivar
An unvarying plant variety, maintained by vegetative propagation or by inbred seed.

Cutting
A piece of plant without roots; set in a rooting medium, a cutting develops roots and can then be potted as a new plant.

Dead-heading
The process of removing spent blooms.

Deciduous
Of leaves, falling off at the end of the growing season; not evergreen.

Disbudding
The pinching off of selected buds to benefit those left to grow.

Disk flower
The small tubular flowers in the central part of a floral head, as in most members of the daisy family. Also called a disk floret.

Division
Propagation of a plant by separating it into two or more pieces, each of which has at least one bud and some roots.

Double-flowered
Having more than the usual number of petals; these extra petals are usually arranged in extra rows.

Drooping
Pendant or hanging, as in the branches of a weeping willow.

Evergreen
Retaining green leaves on one year's growth until after the new leaves for the subsequent year have been formed.

Eye
A bud on a cutting, tuber, or tuberous root.

Fall
One of the sepals of an iris flower, usually drooping.

Fertile
Capable of producing flowers with functional pistils and capable of sexual reproduction.

Floret
One of many very small flowers in a dense flower cluster, especially in the flower heads of the daisy family.

Fruit
The mature, fully developed ovary of a flower, and anything that matures with it, usually one or more seeds.

Genus
A group of closely related species; plural, genera.

Germinate
To sprout (applied to seeds).

Herb
A plant that lacks a permanent, woody stem, and that usually dies back to ground level during cold weather. May be annual or perennial.

Herbaceous perennial
A plant that dies back to ground level each fall, and that sends out new shoots and flowers for several successive years.

Horticulture
The cultivation of plants for ornament or food.

Humus
Partly or wholly decomposed vegetable matter; an important constituent of garden soil.

Hybrid
The offspring of two parent plants that belong to different clones, species, subspecies, or genera.

Invasive
Spreading aggressively from the original site of planting.

Lateral bud
A bud borne in the axil of a leaf or branch, but not at the tip.

Leaflet
One of the subdivisions of a compound leaf, resembling a leaf but not having a bud in its axil.

Loam
A humus-rich soil containing up to 25 percent clay, up to 50 percent silt, and less than 50 percent sand.

Lobe
A segment of a cleft leaf or petal.

Midrib
The mid-vein of a leaf or leaflet; the continuation of the petiole.

Mulch
A protective covering spread over the soil around the base of plants to retard evaporation, control temperature, or enrich the soil.

Naturalized
Having become established in the local flora. Also, of a planting, tended in such a way as to produce the appearance of spontaneous or "wild" growth.

Neck
A thin extension at the apex of some bulbs or tuberous roots.

Neutral soil
Soil that is neither acid nor alkaline, having a pH value of 7.

Node
The place on a stem where a leaf, bud, or branch is attached.

Offset
A short, lateral shoot, ending in an erect bud, and arising at or near the base of a plant; an offset readily produces new roots.

Peat moss
Partly decomposed sphagnum moss, with a high water retention capacity, used as a component of artificial soil mixtures, as a soil amendment, and sometimes as a mulch.

Perennial
A plant whose life span extends over several growing seasons and that produces seeds in several growing seasons, rather than only one. See also Annual and Biennial.

Petal
One of a series of flower parts lying within the sepals and outside the stamens or pistils; often large and brightly colored.

Petiole
The stalk of a leaf.

pH
A symbol for the hydrogen ion content of soil, and thus a means of expressing the acidity or alkalinity of the soil.

Pistil
The female reproductive organ of a flower, consisting of an ovary, style, and stigma.

Pollen
Minute grains containing the male germ cells and produced by the stamens.

Propagate
To produce new plants, either by vegetative means involving the rooting of pieces of a plant, or by sowing seeds.

Raceme
A long flower cluster with a central stalk bearing several smaller individual stalks, each of which produces a flower.

Ray flower
In the daisy family, a flower at the edge of a flowerhead, usually bearing a conspicuous, straplike ray.

Rhizomatous
Having rhizomes.

Rhizome
A horizontal stem at or just below the surface of the ground, distinguished from a true root by the presence of nodes, and often enlarged by food storage.

Rootstock
A rhizome.

Rosette
A crowded cluster of leaves; usually basal, circular, and at ground level.

Runner
A prostrate shoot, rooting at its nodes.

Scale
A small, modified leaf, usually covering a bud or at the base of a pedicel. In true bulbs, the scales are leaf bases, swollen with stored food.

Seed
A fertilized, ripened ovule, almost always covered with a protective coating and contained in a fruit.

Sepal
One of the outermost series of flower parts, arranged in a ring outside the petals, and usually green and leaflike.

Solitary
Borne single or alone; not in clusters.

Spathe
A bract or pair of bracts, often large, that encloses the flowers in certain plants, such as members of the amaryllis family.

Species
A population of plants or animals whose members are potentially able to breed with each other, and which is reproductively isolated from other populations.

Spike
An elongated flower cluster bearing individual flowers that lack stalks.

Spine
A strong, sharp, usually woody projection that takes the place of a leaf on a stem, and which has a bud in its axil.

Stamen
The male reproductive organ of a flower, consisting of a filament and a pollen-containing anther.

Standard
An iris petal, usually erect. See also Fall.

Sterile
Lacking functional stamens or pistils, and therefore not capable of sexual reproduction.

Subspecies
A naturally occurring geographical variant of a species.

Taproot
The main, central vertical root of a plant.

Terminal bud
A bud borne at the tip of a stem or shoot, rather than in a leaf axil.

Terminal raceme
A raceme borne at the tip of the main stem of a plant.

Terminal spike
A spike borne at the tip of the main stem of a plant.

Throat
The opening between the bases of the corolla lobes of a flower, leading into the corolla tube.

Toothed
Having the margin shallowly divided into small, toothlike segments.

Tuber
A swollen, horizontal, mostly underground stem that bears buds and serves as a storage site for food.

Tuberous root
A swollen root used for food storage.

Variety
A population of plants that differ consistently from the typical form of the species, occurring naturally in a geographical area. The term is also popularly applied to forms produced in cultivation.

Vegetative propagation
Propagation by means other than seed.

Whorl
A group of three or more leaves or shoots that all emerge from a stem at a single node.

Wing
A thin, flat extension found at the margins of a seed or leafstalk or along the stem.

PHOTO CREDITS

William Aplin, 89

Gillian Beckett, 38, 46, 59, 86, 88

Sonja Bullaty and Angelo Lomeo ©, Cover, 2, 25

Thomas E. Eltzroth, 64

Derek Fell, 27, 48, 55, 72, 73, 76, 91, 93, 94, 100, 102, 104

Charles Marden Fitch, 87, 90

Pamela J. Harper, 26, 30, 31, 32, 33, 34, 35, 36, 37, 39, 40, 41, 42, 44, 49, 52, 53, 54, 56, 57, 60, 65, 66, 67, 69, 70, 74, 77, 78, 79, 81, 83, 85, 95, 97, 98

Walter H. Hodge, 43, 45, 63, 81, 68, 80, 103

Lee Lockwood, 96, 99, 101

Malak Photographs Ltd., 84

Edward A. McRae, 62

Gary Mottau, 28

Joy Spurr, 47, 50

Steven M. Still, 29, 58, 61, 82

George Taloumis, 71, 75, 92

Thomas K. Todsen, 51

INDEX

CHANTICLEER PRESS
STEWART, TABORI & CHANG

Publisher
ANDREW STEWART

Senior Editor
ANN WHITMAN

Production
KATHY ROSENBLOOM
KARYN SLUTSKY

Design
JOSEPH RUTT